How t
People

Understanding the Human Mind, Psychology, Behavior and Body Language

By Edwin Lee

Copyright 2018 - All rights reserved.

The contents of this book may not be reproduced, duplicated or transmitted without direct written permission from the author. Under no circumstances will any legal responsibility or blame be held against the publisher for any reparation, damages, or monetary loss due to the information herein, either directly or indirectly.

Legal Notice:

This book is copyright protected. This is only for personal use. You cannot amend, distribute, sell, use, quote or paraphrase any part or the content of this book without the consent of the author.

Disclaimer Notice:

Please note the information contained within this document is for educational and entertainment purposes only. Every attempt has been made to provide accurate, up to date and reliable complete information. No warranties of any kind are expressed or implied. Readers acknowledge that the author is not engaging in the rendering of legal, financial, medical or professional advice. The content of this book has been derived from various sources. Please consult a licensed professional before attempting any techniques outlined in this book.

By reading this document, the reader agrees that under no circumstances is the author responsible for any losses, direct or indirect, which are incurred as a result of the use of information contained within this document, including, but not limited to, —errors, omissions, or inaccuracies

© 2018 Edwin Lee

Table of Contents

Introduction 6

Chapter One: Basics to Analyze or Read People ..10

    History of analyzing and manipulating 11

    Art of analyzing people 12

Chapter Two: Understanding the Human Mind ..21

    Freud's model of the human mind 22

        Conscious Mind 23

        Subconscious Mind 24

        Unconscious Mind 24

Chapter Three: Dimensions of Human Mind 29

    Boredom 30

    Fear 31

    Hatred 33

    Joy 35

    Love 36

    Sexuality 38

Chapter Four: Human Behavior and Psychology 41

    What is behavior? 42

        Actions 42

        Cognitions 43

        Emotions 43

    Things to know about human behavior 45

    How to understand the human behavior? 50

Chapter Five: The Psychology of Body Language 56

    Body language and Psychology 57

    Power of the human brain 60

    Interesting facts on Human Psychology 61

Conclusion 67

Additional material 69

Introduction

I want to thank you for purchasing this book: "How to Analyze People - Understanding the Human Mind, Psychology, Behavior and Body Language."

It is true that we consciously or subconsciously try to read another person's mind to know what they are thinking. This process of analyzing people isn't taught to us but comes naturally. Since ancient times, humans have been trying to understand their fellow human beings by focusing on verbal as well as nonverbal cues. But it is not an easy task to analyze a person accurately. To do so, one needs to be logical and practical in their concepts and approach.

If you want to understand a person – be it your spouse, colleague, rival, boss or friend, you will first need to be fair in your thought process. You cannot be biased or allow emotions to ride on your thoughts. For instance, if you don't like your boss, your conscious and subconscious mind will never try to appreciate or accept him (even though he might be right about something). It is necessary to bring down some walls and let go of the narrow-minded thinking. Intellectuality matters the most. People who are learning to read others first learn to read the unseen in themselves. This is one of the most fundamental aspects when it comes to analyzing others.

"to know thyself is the beginning of wisdom" -- Socrates

Be prepared to use your super *spider* senses and look through the person – read all the nonverbal cues. Look for the tiniest details. Pay attention to the body language. Obviously, you will not be able to get everything right overnight. This indeed requires a lot of work. Don't worry though, reading this book grants you a huge head start. So, it is better to first experiment on yourself. Learn more about yourself, analyze your imperfections, and understand your strengths. It is essential to free yourself from the captivity of your own negative thoughts and unreal assumptions. Introspect. Once you see success, you can try to implement it on your close ones (friends, family, etc.).

"we must know thyself and thy enemy" – Sun Tzu

The human brain is a powerful and interesting organ. Scientists and mind readers are still studying this organ to try and understand why and how it does certain things. The conscious and subconscious part of the human mind plays a significant role in our behavior and personality. Unfortunately, a majority of us have little to no understanding of how they work.

It is difficult to understand the human mind completely since it is very delicate and complex. This is the reason different thinkers have defined it in different ways. Freud's model of the human mind is the base of all theories. In 1900, Sigmund Freud originally defined the structure of the human mind and its personality. Almost all psychologists, psychiatrists, mind readers and mentalists still follow the topographical model he defined.

This book will give you information on how to analyze people and understand their behavior and psychology. Understanding the complex set of characteristics and emotions in a person is a challenging task indeed. However, mastering this hidden art gives you great benefits. Learning to analyze others is more important than ever. Living in the digital world we've come to forget the fundamental interaction, its hidden variables, and most importantly, ourselves. If you've the ability to read others like an open book, you'll have huge edge in every aspect of life. As experts say, don't limit or restrict yourself to specific protocols and theories.

The chapters in this book will help you understand more about the human mind, psychology, and behavior.

Thank you once again for buying this book. I hope it serves you well as an informative and interesting read!

Happy Reading!

"A reader lives thousand lives before he dies, said Jojen. The man who never reads lives only one."

-– George R.R. Martin

Chapter One: Basics to Analyze or Read People

Isn't analyzing or reading people a psychiatrist's forte? Why would I do that? Well, even without a degree, an average person tries to analyze every other fellow being he or she comes across. The moment a human bumps into a fellow being, he or she starts to analyze the body language, the eye contact, the body posture and the voice tone. He or she tries to find the real person behind the mask one usually wears. This can be done only when one can interpret both verbal and nonverbal cues.

It is not always possible to go by logic – it won't tell you the complete story about a person. It is important to analyze all the other critical information that people give you in the form of nonverbal signals. If you want to do this, then the first thing to keep in mind is to get rid of all the preconceived notions and assumptions you have. Leave all your emotional baggage behind. Let go of the ego clashes, anger and old resentments. These emotional factors stop you from being able to see a person clearly. The primary aspect is to stay objective and receive information without disturbing or distorting it. Be neutral.

History of analyzing and manipulating

Throughout the history it has been one the most important skills to learn and master. Being able to analyze people has allowed rapid success through all the different ages. Ever since the first civilizations were built, people had the need to analyze each other. Ancient Egypt, Babylon, Greece, Rome, Middle Ages, Renaissance etc. we've always been curious to know what others are up to. Especially those seeking for success (relative), it has been mandatory to interact and understand the competition. Although we do not practice manipulation directly in this book, it has always played big part in our lives, and being able to analyze others plays a significant part in all human psychology. During the era. Of Greece philosophers like Socrates, Plato, Aristotle, and many others formed many of the very basic ideas of human psychology we know today. Also, those in power were obligated to carefully analyze everyone they met. Imagine you were the king of the court. You could never rest. There was always the need to be aware against all types of assassinations, manipulation, and freeloaders. The courts and palaces were one of the prime examples in the history of "mind games".

Art of analyzing people

Art is a form of creativity. Analyzing or reading people is an art. We have often times lost the natural touch of hidden nonverbal cues due to the rising interaction online. However, think creatively and tweak these techniques and you might even analyze people online! As a matter of a fact that could one additional way to begin. Look up different people's body language when you're watching a video etc. You need to be broad-minded and think out of the box. There are the three basic techniques to read people:

- Examine the body language
- Pay attention to your intuition
- Feel the emotional energy and nonverbal expressions

Examine the body language signals

According to research, our communication is a combination of words, voice tone, and body language. Only **seven percent** of communication is represented by words, and the remaining 93 percent is split into the tone of voice (38 percent) and body language (55 percent). Don't try too hard to concentrate on one's body language – you need to relax and let it go. Getting excessively analytical or intense will result in you missing the simple and important body language signs. Relax. Sit back, get comfortable and just observe!

Appearance

While you are trying to analyze people, pay attention to their appearance – their presentation and dress style. If you come across a person who wears polished shoes and a power suit, he or she is dressed for success. Perhaps they are ambitious! Again, this depends on the scenario. If he or she is going to meet the executives or the top management, this attire is called for. But if you see them dressed like this on normal days or when you are meeting them for the first time, then yes – there are signals to be understood.

If the person is in a t-shirt and jeans, then it indicates comfort and a casual demeanor. Similarly, if a woman wears a tight top accentuating her bosom, it is considered a seductive choice. Someone with a Buddha pendant or with a religious symbol might indicate that he or she gives importance to religious or spiritual values.

Check the body posture

While reading the body posture, try to question your observations before coming to a conclusion. Are they confident just because they are holding their head high? Will cowering while walking be considered a sign of low self-esteem? Puffed out chest with a hint of arrogance – perhaps ego? Read the environment and then decide. For instance, at some occasions, you can even directly estimate how much time a person spends sedentary, based on their crouched posture.

Observe the physical movements

Check how the person leans when he or she is involved in a conversation. Proximity matters a lot. How close or far are they while interacting? When you like someone, you tend to lean towards them. But when you don't, you lean away from them.

Crossed legs or arms suggest a defensive or blocking posture. It can also mean anger or that a person is reserved in nature. While crossing legs, people usually point their toes towards the person they are comfortable with.

Keeping hands inside the pockets, on the lap or behind the back might indicate that they are either nervous or uncomfortable. It may also mean that they are hiding something.

People tend to pick their cuticles or bite their lips when they are in an awkward situation. Some do this to calm themselves when feeling scared or under pressure.

<u>Read the facial expression</u>

You may try to control your emotions, but your face will reflect them clearly. Are you thinking too much or worrying about something? The deep frown lines on your forehead are signs. Do you want to know if a person is genuinely smiling? See if you can see the crow's feet or wrinkles near their eyes. Anger, hatred, bitterness or dislikes are evident on a person's face in form of pursed lips. See someone grinding their teeth or with their jaw clenched? Perhaps he or she is trying to control their anger.

Pay attention to your intuition

Sometimes, you can't gauge a person just by listening to their words or observing their body language. Your inner self might be trying to tell you something more. The gut feeling you get when you notice certain people or are in particular scenarios is called intuition. It is not what your head says but what your gut feels (the vibes if you will). This is the nonverbal information you identify through the 'hmms' and 'ahhas' of the person. It is about the images, the environment, and the scenarios. Gut instinct never lies. To understand someone you need to know who he or she really is (without the mask). Intuition helps you read between the lines and see the actual story.

How do I know my intuition is telling me something?

- Respect your intuition. When you meet a person for the first time, observe what your instinct is telling you. Intuition is the primitive feeling or reaction that occurs even before you get a chance to think. The uneasy feeling you get when you meet someone is your gut instinct – the primal response. This will tell you that something is not right.

Decide if you can really trust a person by listening to your gut feeling – it is your internal truth-meter.
- Do you get goosebumps when you are with a person? Do they give you a positive feeling inside? Well, the sign is optimistic. Goosebumps are amazing intuitive tingling sensations that arise when you resonate with people. Why? Because these people inspire you in some way. You might be able to strike a chord with them. You get goosebumps when you experience the feeling of déjà vu. It is an odd feeling that makes you feel that you know the person, though you might not have actually met before.
- Do you get flashes of insights the moment you see someone or when you interact with someone? Like a bulb going on inside your head with the "aha" expression? It comes in a flash. You need to really stay attentive or you will miss it. If you get such sensations - never allow the person into your life.
- Do you feel an intense form of empathy when you meet a person? Perhaps because of the physical appearance or the emotion displayed by the person? Sometimes you tend to get upset or depressed after a meeting. This

might be because you empathize with the person, and understand their circumstances.

Feel the emotional energy

The dramatic expression of our energy can be termed as emotions. It is the vibe that you give off. One's gut feeling or inner guidance helps you understand or register these emotions. For instance, you may feel good and positive when you are around certain people. They have the power to improve your mood in an instant. Their mere presence can give you energy. But there are few who can emotionally drain you. Whenever you see such people, all you feel is the need to disappear.

You will be able to feel these subtle energies within inches of the body – like invisible vibrations. The Chinese call this the chi of the body – the vital energy, necessary for good health.

Is it possible to read these emotional energies? Do we have strategies to help us do that? Yes, we do! Let's look at them now:

Sensing the emotional presence of the people

There is an overall energy we usually emit – this energy need not reflect in our behavior or words. But there is an emotional air that surrounds us, like the sun or rain or the cloud. It is around us! Observe if the person whom you are analyzing has a friendly charisma, which attracts you? Or do you get bad vibes that make you turn away from the person?

Observe the eyes

Eye contact is critical when it comes to analyzing people. Even when words or facial expressions fail, eyes can end up giving you a lot of information. Our eyes send out powerful energies. Studies have shown that eyes project electromagnetic signal, which the brain usually extends beyond the body. Spend time in observing one's eyes. What is it that you see in them? What is the emotion they display? Anger? Joy? Tranquility? Meanness? Seductiveness? Grief? You can also sense if their eyes are fixed on someone. Do they feel at home when they think of someone? Sign of intimacy? Or are they hiding something? Guarding a secret?

Perceive the feel of physical touch

Psychological feelings are conveyed through physiological gestures. The emotional energy we feel can be shared with others through physical contact. When you are overjoyed, you feel the urge to hug someone you like. Similarly, try to observe the physical touch of other people. Was the handshake with your boss comfortable or was it too dominating? Did the hug from your colleague feel warm, confident and genuine? Or did it put you off so much that you wanted to withdraw immediately? When you shake hands with people, you might often notice that for some it is sweaty or too rigid or floppy. Sweaty hands might signal tension or anxiety. Rigid hands indicate confidence or professionalism. Floppy hands might suggest shyness or non-commitment.

Voice tone and laughter matters

Your voice tone and volume speak volumes about the emotions you are experiencing. The voice tone can help you sense the vibes being transmitted by a person. The frequencies of the sound create vibrations – so voice tone definitely matters! Some people have a voice tone that gives you a soothing feeling. You will feel happy listening to them. You will want to hear more of their voice. Some others might have a rough, unpleasant or shrill tone.

In course of the next few chapters, we will be getting into details of the role of the human brain, its behavior and the psychology behind it. This will help us learn how to analyze people.

Chapter Two: Understanding the Human Mind

The intent of psychoanalytic theory is to understand the human mind. Sigmund Freud was the first person to introduce a theory on the human mind in the early 1900s. Although there have been many advancements in the study of psychoanalytic theory, the thoughts shared by Freud about the theory of human mind is still considered the primary foundation.

Freud divided the human mind into three levels and had quoted the estimated usage of the mind on each level as

- Conscious (10 %)
- Subconscious (50 to 60%)
- Unconscious (30 to 40%)

All these three levels work together to create our reality. Did you know that the word 'mind' has a rich and long history? This particular word doesn't have any clear evolution when compared to the other phrases and words in the English language. The meaning of the word 'mind' depends more on the context of its usage than as an individual word.

For instance, the word mind might indicate a person's identity, personality and memories when a philosopher uses it. When the word is used in religious context, it can mean that the mind is a spirit (awareness of God). For a scientist, the mind is a thought-generator or a place where he gets his ideas. The mind has carried many different labels, and the ancient references look abstract in this case.

After the 14th and 15th centuries, the term mind was generalized to include all mental related abilities – feeling, memory, thought, decision, etc. Psychology was considered a respected form of science in the late 19th and early 20th century. Due to the work of Freud and many others, more focus was given to the human mind, the role it plays in behavioral science and the mind-body coordination. They had set a strong foundation that led to discussions on the concept of mind from a scientific point of view.

Freud's model of the human mind

Sigmund Freud had segregated the human mind into three levels:

- Conscious Mind
- Subconscious Mind
- Unconscious Mind

Conscious Mind

When you are aware of what is happening to you and around you, it means you are in a conscious state. Conscious mind would refer to the part of the mind that is able to recall the earlier activities and events. The two important challenges to this point of view is that

- Only ten percent of the mind holds conscious thoughts and works on them.
- It cannot explain the random events that are created inside the mind.

The two primary tasks that the conscious mind has the capability of handling are:

- Ability to focus or concentrate
- Ability to imagine things that are not real

The conscious mind, an important part that works in harmony with the human mind, is basically a scanner for us. It helps by performing the following:

- Recognizes an event
- Initiates trigger if there is a need to react
- Stores the event (depending on the significance of the event)
- The storage can happen either in the subconscious or unconscious area of the

human mind (as it is then permanently available there)

Subconscious Mind

The storage point for you to quickly recall any recent memories or events is in the subconscious mind. For instance, if you need to recall the name of the person you met a week ago or the mobile number you just heard, your subconscious mind helps you in getting the information. This level of the mind holds all the current information that you use on a daily basis – your habits, feelings, behavioral patterns and frequent thoughts. Freud's subconscious mind acts as the mind's RAM (random access memory). This is one reliable workhorse of the mind-body experience.

Unconscious Mind

All our memories and past experiences live in the unconscious mind. These memories might have been consciously forgotten - thoughts that are no longer important, generic automatic thoughts and incidents suppressed through trauma or pain. These experiences and memories are the reason for the formation of our habits, beliefs, and behaviors.

The unconscious mind is effectively the:

- Warehouse of memories long gone

- Source of random thoughts and dreams
- Center point of implicit understanding and knowledge

These old memories might still be accessible to the conscious mind at some point in our life. Similarly, these random thoughts may appear without any particular reason or obvious cause. The implicit knowledge stored in the unconscious mind helps us do things we have learned so well that we don't need to rethink while doing them.

You can now consider the unconscious mind as the cellar – the underground repository of information. All your memories, behaviors and habits are there. It is the storeroom that holds all the emotions that you've experienced since birth.

Modern psychology has opened itself to many new theories and ideas based on the Freudian theory. Freud's psychoanalytical theory is definitely worth studying, to understand a critical chronological perspective of mental health treatment.

Human mind

There has been a new debate in recent times in which researchers and thinkers have suggested that there's a balance between the conscious and unconscious mind. What do they mean? It is a way of saying that the conscious mind is the part due to which we are aware of what is happening in the present moment, and unconscious mind is the part where the other things (that don't pop up right now) are stored. Let's not forget that we only have one mind – these are just layers within it.

An example might help you to understand this better. Let us say you are driving home using the usual route. You realize that for the last few minutes your mind has not been on the road. As you enter the neighborhood, you wonder how you even managed to get close to home without properly concentrating on taking the right turns, minding the traffic signals, watching out for other vehicles, etc. The point is you had been daydreaming and still got to your destination. Therefore, it can be understood that there are still a number of things you can do even while you aren't paying proper attention to them all the time. Your mind is able to pick up the necessary memories and guide you on to the right path. The mind doesn't face any difficulty in swinging between its various levels to create awareness.

The inference from this example can be that the subconscious mind processes all the necessary information with conscious awareness. Hence, it is the subconscious mind, which has taken control here. For instance, when we are looking at a bird flying, the conscious mind (the result of cognitive processing) tells us that the bird is not going to fall and is safe in the sky. But the underlying subconscious mind (inclusive of the unconscious mind) processes information such as the bird's movement, distance, color, form, identity, etc. Though we see it as a whole event – a white bird flying high (at a considerably long distance), our conscious mind is more focused on the motion (flying).

There were a few psychologists from the modern West who started talking about the universal and the super conscious parts of the mind. Indian philosophers, thinkers and researchers already accepted these notion ages ago. But since Freud's theory did not support collective unconscious (which was mentioned by Jung), the transpersonal part of the mind had been ignored for years. But Jung already had a firm opinion that it is the unconscious mind of the human, which gives him or her all the help and encouragement when he or she needs it.

"It holds possibilities which are locked away from the conscious mind, for it has at its disposal all subliminal psychic contents, all those things which

have been forgotten or overlooked, as well as the wisdom and experience of uncounted centuries which are laid down in its archetypal organs.... The unconscious can serve man as a unique guide, provided he can resist the lure of being misguided."

The super conscious mind can be referred to as the mind of the soul. So, what do we conclude then? It is important that you don't get confused by the terms conscious, subconscious and unconscious. They are nothing but levels of the mind, used to describe certain functionalities.

- The Conscious mind gives you thoughts that you are aware of.
- The Subconscious mind has all the old habits, emotions, memories, etc. which can be recalled whenever needed. The subconscious mind is the key for personal change.
- The Unconscious mind stores universal thoughts and experiences, the forgotten memories, long-gone instincts, etc

Each of these is accessible to us in a way since they already communicate with one another. It is, therefore, necessary to try and develop a mind, which can observe and judge by using all the stored information in conscious, subconscious and unconscious layers.

Chapter Three: Dimensions of Human Mind

The human mind operates under six fundamental dimensions, and the intensity of these dimensions helps in deriving human behavior or characteristics. Understanding these dimensions is essential if you wish to be able to analyze others. The following six dimensions are applicable to all human minds:

- Boredom
- Fear
- Hatred
- Joy
- Love
- Sexuality

It is impossible to completely erase these dimensions from the mind. Ever heard your friend saying, *"I will never love again because the feeling will never come"*? The person thinks he is trying to erase the emotion (i.e., the dimension) from the mind but, unfortunately, that is not possible. You can only suppress your mind, which will ultimately lead to resistance. This inner resistance will manifest as suffering in one form or another.

For instance, some people misinterpret or get the wrong notion of certain spiritual teachings and try to repress certain dimensions in their mind, such as fear, sexuality or hatred. This will result in them fighting a constant battle with their minds; a battle which might last their entire lives.

It is important to understand consciously that the mind is powerful. When you try to impose divine or religious restraints on it, you will not be able to experience them completely. When you cease such attempts, you will no longer be opposing or battling your mind's natural dimensions. This will give you a pleasant experience.

Let's get into the details of the six dimensions of the human mind.

Boredom

When the mind lacks interest in the current moment, you tend to get bored. It is basically a state of darkness in the mind. Boredom is nothing to really worry about. But continuous boredom can lead to depression. This dimension of the mind encourages it to chase creative things, pursue new aspirations and entertain the physical life. Boredom can help provide growth and interest in things you had long forgotten or stopped pursuing due to lack of time.

When you feel bored, don't suppress the feeling. Allow it to flow, and get the real sensation of boredom. Experience it to the fullest. Don't run away from boredom or get scared of it. Embracing the energy of boredom in true sense can give you peace and calm. When you are bored, you tend to do things that you like such as reading, painting, listening to music, singing, walking in the woods, listening to the birds, admiring the nature, etc. When you don't resist it, it can bring joy to your mind.

Boredom can help balance the state of extreme excitement, which is sometimes necessary to maintain harmony with the body's energy.

Fear

Fear is the state of darkness in the mind. All human minds get to feel this dimension. Some people experience fear more than others, and this depends on the natural make-up of the dimensions in the human mind. A mind that is fearful can create resistance to your movements on a constant basis. It is definitely a big source of disturbance. Suppressing this dimension (fear) of the mind is impossible.

As you become conscious of your fears, you can stop getting scared of the mind's fears, i.e., stop recognizing the mind's fears and just let them be (perhaps ignore them). When the mind has a strong inclination towards fear, it will keep generating fear-based thoughts. But when you stop providing fuel to this state of mind, it will start losing its intensity and power to influence your vibes. You will no longer be dominated by fear.

Fear is a powerful catalyst that can push you to wake up – it gives you the sense of awakening. What are the different forms of fear?

- Anxiety
- Guilt
- Horror
- Panic
- Worry
- Depression
- Concern
- Insecurity
- Guilt
- Obsession
- Restlessness

- Negative excitement
- Nervousness

Which of these do you experience most often? A human mind can never be completely free of fear, as the dimension is deep-rooted inside it. So, you should not worry about stopping your mind from generating fear. But you should create a conscious awareness to identify fear and ensure you are no longer influenced by it. Great way to practice this is by simple meditation.

Hatred

Similar to boredom and fear, hatred is also a state of darkness in the mind. This dimension can be found in all human minds and plays a major role in deciding one's likes and dislikes (the preferences, in general).

You can never get away from hatred – this dimension is deeply imbibed in the mind. If you try to repress the mind when it generates hate based thoughts, then you end up building a lot of repressed negative energy inside. This pent-up energy can be highly toxic for you, and make you dysfunctional.

How does your mind express hatred? Hatred gets expressed in the following ways:

- Anger
- Apathy
- Dissatisfaction
- Aggressiveness
- Suspicion
- Irritation
- Stress
- Jealousy
- Criticism
- Resentment
- Vanity
- Dislike
- Impatience
- Frustration
- Possessiveness
- Inferiority

When you make conscious efforts to understand that hatred is just a dimension of the mind, you work towards 'not making it personal.' You can't change the past but just let the mind flow, i.e., you don't identify it individually. You don't give energy to the hate-based thoughts and simply allow the mind to generate them. The moment you try to suppress them, you indirectly end up giving attention to them by fueling the emotion.

Don't judge yourself for the thoughts your mind produces – just let them be. When you don't give them energy, they won't have the intensity to influence your mind.

Joy

This dimension is the light nature of the mind – the natural vibration of life energy. It vibrates with the positivity of who you basically are. The mind gets aligned with its life-stream whenever it gets into the state of joy.

When a person is in a joyful state, the body feels good and there is no internal or external resistance. This is why everyone wants to feel joyful! Joy can be expressed in the following ways:

- Enthusiasm
- Excitement
- Calm
- Peace
- Exhilaration
- Sensual pleasure (enjoying touch, sight, sound, smell, and taste)

The capacity to feel joy is present inside every human mind, but there are differences in how each experiences the dimension. Certain minds are more attracted to peace – their expression of joy would be serenity and relaxation. Some minds prefer boisterous and energetic expressions such as enthusiasm, excitement and exhilaration. But there is generally a balance where we would like both the excitement and peace in equal combinations.

This dimension of the mind will definitely need to be expressed. Some people suppress their joy because they fear it won't last long. Some shy away from joy due to guilt or imagine they will suffer. Joy is a natural vibration of life energy, and therefore it is important to allow your mind the opportunity to properly experience this dimension. You need to be wise enough not to go overboard or overindulge in things you shouldn't be doing.

Love

Similar to joy, love is another light nature of the mind. All the human minds have this dimension in them. The mind expresses love in various forms, such as,

- Devotion
- Care
- Service
- Passion
- Infatuation

- Empathy
- Obsession (based on love)
- Compassion
- Charity
- Romance (both emotional and physical)
- Tenderness

It is possible for every human mind to hold all these expressions of love. Most humans usually express almost all the forms of love in one way or the other. When the mind feels secure, it has more capacity for love.

But unfortunately, the dimension of love can also become a source of dissonance and imbalance in the mind when it is in the state of unconsciousness.

For instance, if you are obsessed with someone or something that your mind is in love with, the patterns of obsession can lead to insecurity, possessiveness, neediness and various other aspects of fear. Similarly, when passion is not balanced, then it can lead to wantonness and over-indulgence. It is essential to control and balance the emotion with maturity or through wisdom else you can become a prisoner to the thing or person you love.

Therefore it is equally possible for the dimension of love to go into an imbalance mode when you lack consciousness. Being aware in the present (i.e. meditation) helps to hold the balance.

Sexuality

This dimension can be categorized as a dark aspect of the mind. This is because of the heaviness involved in this energy. Like every other dimension, all human minds have this dimension. When it is not understood or channelized in the right manner, it can lead to frustration, depravity, hang-ups and guilt.

It is this dimension in the mind that is responsible for human reproduction – it causes the movement toward the reproductive phase. Therefore, this dimension plays an imperative role in the physical realm. Sexuality gives pleasure and entertainment to the mind. It is also a way through which you can express joy and love. Suppressing sexuality is not a good idea as it can cause disharmony and toxicity in the human body. The energy of sexuality can be intense and hence suppressing this dimension in the mind due to guilt or fear can lead to patterns of hatred inside. The patterns of hatred usually take the form of anger.

All people have their own drive toward their sexuality – this can change with age, i.e., can either increase or decrease. Therefore, you need to be aware and mindful about not indulging in too much of it or suppressing it once and for all. It is true that all the other dimensions of the mind directly affect the dimension of sexuality.

For example, when your mind is completely overcome by fear, you don't get interested in sex. Similarly, when the mind is full of hatred, sexuality has no place there. Boredom is also a good reason for declining sex. On the other hand, the dimensions of joy and love can lead to a healthy sex drive.

The crucial and important thing one needs to understand is that these dimensions are hard-wired into the mind. Therefore, it is not possible to completely erase them from the human mind. These dimensions will be displayed possibly on a day-to-day basis as long as the mind is healthy and alive.

Most humans are fine with the light nature of the mind, such as joy and love but don't make any attempts to understand the dark natured dimensions of the mind. Boredom, hatred, fear and sexuality can become unhealthy dimensions if you show patterns of opposition and suppression toward their nature. It is important to understand these dimensions and focus on working towards understanding them instead of oppressing them.

When there is stability in your awareness, you will be able to freely express all the dimensions without getting dominated by them. When this happens, your vibrations no longer show any negative influence related to these dimensions of the mind. This state of true freedom allows you to experience holistic physicality.

Chapter Four: Human Behavior and Psychology

Most researchers are looking to get a deeper understanding of human behavior – the way humans act, memorize, make decisions and plan, etc. In recent times, there have been tremendous advancements in sensor technology with processes for data analysis and acquisition. These have been helping researchers all over the globe to unravel the secrets of the human mind.

Though there are a lot of challenges involved in the process, they are trying to observe and interpret the processes of the human brain that can ultimately help in analyzing the cognition and changes in behavior.

Humans are active agents who are constantly engaged in trying to fulfill all their mental desires and bodily needs. They ensure this is done when they are interacting with the environment even though the surroundings keep changing with growing complexity. The bodily behaviors are evolved through the cognitive processing that happens in the brain structures.

What is behavior?

Scientific research suggests that the human behavior is a complex interaction between the three components:

- Actions (Act)
- Cognitions (Think)
- Emotions (Feel)

Does it sound complicated? To make it simple, you need to understand that actions, cognitions and emotions are components of human behavior. When these three work together, the final result is the behavior or characteristic of the person.

Actions

An action denotes anything and everything that can be perceived or observed. The observation can either be measured by the physiological sensors or through the naked eye. You can imagine action to be a state of transition from one mode to another. It can also mean the initiation of a particular mode. For example, when a director is getting ready to film the next scene in his movie, he shouts action, i.e., he is asking the artists to move from their real state to reel state (acting mode).

Behavioral actions take place on different scales – these can range from muscular activation to consuming food, sleep, the activity of the sweat glands, etc.

Cognitions

The thoughts and the images you hold in your mind can be described through cognition. They can be both nonverbal and verbal. *'I have to remember to take my pills before I go to bed'* or *'I would like to know what he thinks of me'* – are verbal cognition. When you imagine how your new house will look after the construction is completed, it is considered nonverbal cognition.

Cognitions consist of knowledge and skills. For instance, knowing how to use the gardening tools properly without getting hurt, dancing to the tunes of your favorite song, memorizing the color of the hat a musician is wearing in an album, etc.

Emotions

Emotions are behaviors that exist on a scale – from positive (pleasing) to negative (unlikeable). An emotion is a feeling that cannot be characterized by knowledge or logical reasoning. It is a brief conscious experience that is identified by an intense mental activity.

The physiological aspects of the human body, which indicate the processing of emotions, are not visible to the eyes directly. For instance, increased arousal can result in high respiration rate or heart rate. These emotions cannot be directly observed. It is possible to spot these emotions by the following different methods:

- Respiration sensors
- ECG (to monitor arousal)
- Analyzing facial expressions
- Tracking the facial electromyography activity (FEMG)
- Galvanic skin response (GSR), etc.

You need to understand that everything is connected – action, cognition and emotion. They don't run independently and continuously interact with each other. If these three components interact well with each other, it enables you as a human to recognize the world around you, respond to the people and stimuli in the environment appropriately and listen to your inner desires.

But it is quite difficult to finalize on the cause and effect of these behaviors. We will try to explain this with an example.

You turn your head (<u>action</u>) and see a familiar face which causes a sudden explosion of joy (<u>emotion</u>). This is accompanied by a realization (<u>cognition</u>). The actions, in this case, are you seeing someone you know (a friend) and feeling happy.

Action = Cognition (hey, Thomas!) + Emotion (joy of seeing Thomas)

In a different case, the sequence of cause and effect can get reversed. For example,

You decide to go for a walk (<u>action</u>) to feel better because you are sad (<u>emotion</u>) and have been thinking deeply about your relationship problems (<u>cognition</u>).

Action = Cognition (I need to go for a walk) + Emotion (feeling sad)

Things to know about human behavior

Sensory impressions are more important to humans – you get actively involved in persuading your body to experience the emotional states. If the emotion is positive, you experience joy, but when the emotion is negative, you want to get out of the negativity. This is achieved by the cognitive desires and goals your mind makes (consciously or unconsciously).

Though you cannot directly observe emotion and cognition, you can certainly feel the final execution through the action. For instance, you are bored (emotion), and you think you need to watch a movie (cognition) so you go to the theatre (action).

You also need to understand that cognition is specific to situation and time. Any new information or data you experience gets integrated into your already existing cognitive mindset. This information is adapted and merged with your cognitive ability. You are now able to predict the turn of events based on the current environment and how your action will influence the same. So, when you decide to perform an action, you are going to put your plan (decision) into working mode based on the situation and environment.

The dynamic interplay of stability and flexibility of your mind can be managed by your cognitive system.

Abstract cognition and imagination are body-based. What is abstract cognition? This doesn't have any direct physical interaction with the environment. For instance, when you imagine moving your hands, the thought process triggers the same areas of the brain (when they actually execute the hand movements).

Behavioral learning

When we discuss behavior, it is important to know how it is acquired in general. What is learning? The process of acquiring new skills, knowledge, preferences, evaluations, attitude, normative behavior and social rules can be termed learning. Have you heard of the nature-nurture argument? Earlier there was a debate going on about human behavior – is the behavior exclusively driven by environmental factors (nurture) or by genetic inclinations (nature)?

But today, the question no longer exists, as the impact of both nature and nurture are similar on human behavior. Evidence proves that the interplay of both these factors plays a major role in the behavioral pattern. Recent theories highlight the role of learning to acquire new skills and knowledge to develop or change your behavior. The ongoing acquisition of skills all throughout your life will definitely have an impact on the nervous system (at the neurological level).

Practice makes you perfect! The more you learn, the more the changes you see in the behavioral pattern.

<u>Classical Conditioning</u> is one of the learning procedures that helps us learn the stimulus-response pairings. For instance, when you see food that looks tasty, it immediately triggers salivation. 'Whoa, yummy food'! Food acts as the unconditioned stimulus while the salivation process is the unconditioned response to it.

You see food (Unconditioned stimulus) = Salivation (Unconditioned response)

When the food is accompanied by another stimulus (neutral), like the doorbell ringing, the brain learns a new stimulus-response pairing.

You see food (Unconditioned stimulus) and hear the doorbell ring (conditioned stimulus) = Salivation (Unconditioned response).

Why does the bell become a conditioned stimulus? That is because it is powerful enough to trigger salivation even when you haven't seen the food yet.

So, doorbell ringing (conditioned stimulus) = Salivation (Response).

Behavioral Decision-making

Sometimes, decisions and behavior go hand in hand. For instance, you look at the behavior of others and take a decision based on the impact it can have in your life. For example: *'If my colleague gets warned for sending the data, I will definitely not be doing it'!* In this case, you wait for your colleague to send particular data before you do it – you are taking a decision based on the effects of another person's behavior.

When the individual decides to hold back a specific behavior or execute a certain action depending on the associated risks, incentives and benefits, the behavior is actually acquired through learning. But are there any other factors or theories associated with such decision-making?

The most prominent psychological theories on decision-making have their origin in an economics journal. Amos Tversky and Daniel Kahneman published a paper on *The Prospect Theory* in 1979. This theoretical framework helped Daniel Kahneman to study human behavior in the later stages. All his research and findings were summarized in his book Thinking, Fast and Slow. This book went on to become a bestseller.

Emotional Decision-making

One cannot deny the fact that decision-making and human behaviors are largely affected by emotions. You may not always recognize this, but emotions affect the process delicately. When you are emotionally on the higher side and you take a decision, it usually ends up as the worst decision ever. To justify our action, we make use of imperfect reasons.

As Andrade and Ariely rightly pointed out - *"a mild incidental emotion in decision-making can live longer than the emotional experience itself"*

Researchers experimented to understand how a person's mood affected their decision-making skills. They wanted to know if positive feeling can affect a person's readiness to help.

A quarter-cent was placed in a phone booth for passers-by to find. The coin was placed in a visible position. An actor was made to step into the booth requesting to take an urgent phone call when another person was already inside. The people, who found the coin when they went in, were happy to help the actor but those who didn't, gave a negative reply.

How to understand the human behavior?

Many people fail to understand human behavior because they don't take all the other variables, apart from the behavior, into consideration.

For instance, you can never understand a car's wheel unless and until you make the effort to analyze the wheel's relationship with the other parts of the car. Even the most expensive car is made-up from all the different parts. By focusing on the single part you will simply end up failing to understand its functionality on the whole.

If you don't know why wheels have certain holes in the central part, you might end up thinking that the wheel is faulty. But when you understand that these holes in the wheel are necessary for fitting it onto the rotating shaft, everything makes sense.

It is the same for humans. You will never be able to understand human behavior accurately unless you make a conscious effort to look at all the other variables that can directly or indirectly affect the human. These other variables can be – the person's lifestyle, thought-process, beliefs, values, childhood, etc.

Example to help you understand the human behavior:

Paul 25, a self-made millionaire, was a confident, charming and energetic person. He made his first million in vastly quick manner. The man was proud of himself and all of his expensive goods. He often used to identify himself as a 'self-made millionaire.' It sort of became his main psychological identity.

Like on any other day, he parked his Lamborghini in the parking lot dedicated to him and went to his cabin. But on that particular day, he came down several times to check if he had left his car's door unlocked. He kept doing it after every few minutes. He didn't know why he was doing it. He later discovered that he had developed this weird OCD (Obsessive Compulsive Disorder), which forced him to check his car so often.

If you have no idea about human psychology, this behavior will not make any difference to you. You might think that too much stress led to this behavior and the brain chemistry is deteriorating. This is partly true, but it is impossible to analyze this behavior unless you have clarity on his personality.

After that day, for the next couple of weeks, Paul kept dreaming about his car getting stolen. The dream was repetitive. For someone who didn't know much about human nature, this might have seemed like Paul was scared of losing his car and this fear fueled these dreams. Again, this is not the right conclusion!

Paul started facing serious issues in his business due to this OCD, which made him vulnerable – he lost his competency in business. This threatened his most important psychological identity – self-made millionaire. If he completely went out of business, he would lose all the money and the identity of a 'self-made millionaire.'

It is therefore important to analyze one's own behavior clearly and avoid assumptions. Human psychology is a complex aspect of science – only when you are able to understand the behavior and its relation to the brain will you be able to get a solution.

Connecting the elements to understand the human nature better

Paul's dream of losing the car was a reflection of his fear of losing his identity of a 'self-made millionaire.' Dreams are a form of symbolism – they sometimes show you your worst fears! Paul's dream meant that he was concerned about losing his current millionaire status.

The point to be understood here is – the subconscious mind of the human brain uses symbolism to notify the individual of certain things as it ignores logic when it functions. Paul's mind was so concerned about losing his main psychological status that it forced him to develop the obsessive-compulsive disorder.

Psychological inference: Paul developed OCD because he was too scared to lose his millionaire status. The reason for checking if his car was locked more than often reflected his fear of becoming poor. Because, according to him, when you lose your car (luxury Lamborghini), you become poor. This would imply his identity was linked into the physical items rather than the wealth itself.

This is quite common amongst people that win the lottery as well as highly paid actors and athletes. Did you know that roughly 70~% of the lottery winners go broke or back to where they started in just few years? The perceived shift from ordinary to "extraordinary" is often too much for their subconscious mind to handle, and they don't have a clear identity formed. They aren't conscious enough of their own mind and attach to the old identity. Hence 70~% have their identities attached to excessive spending or other similar issue and they keep spending in the same manner as before. Just on a bigger scale. As their liabilities (fancy car, house etc.) exceed the income, they will always run out of money, eventually.

So, whenever you try to understand human behavior, don't just stop at observing a single thing – instead, focus on all the other things in the system. What would you think of a woman who is scared of cats? Perhaps she had an upsetting experience with cats when she was a kid. No, this is a quick assumption. It might not be true. Instead of being quick in concluding, look at the other aspects of her life.

- It can be the fear of other women which is reflecting in this form (fear of cats)
- Perhaps her self-esteem is making her feel vulnerable
- She might not be confident enough to present herself in front of other women, and the subconscious mind is symbolizing these women in the form of cats.

Don't overexert: just always try to take a deeper look to understand the human behavior better. Be creative and don't be afraid to play with many different ideas before coming into conclusion.

Chapter Five: The Psychology of Body Language

People constantly give you a hoard of signals, both verbal and non-verbal. The silent signals coming from the person's body language communicate a lot of meaningful information. Human communication comprises 80 percent nonverbal and 20 percent verbal cues. You need to ensure that whatever you say matches your body language. For instance, you say 'I am fine,' but your jaws are clenched, and your lips pursed; then you are communicating the exact opposite of what you are saying.

Nonverbal cues come in the form of body language – hand gestures, body postures, facial expressions, eye contact, micro-expressions, pupil dilation, voice tone, etc. It is therefore important to communicate your thoughts, feelings and needs through apt and proper body language.

Our ancestors communicated effectively for millions of years and survived in this dangerous world. They were able to communicate their desires, needs and emotions efficiently. And the best part is they never used verbal communication since they didn't have a language. All their communications were through body language, using the nonverbal cues.

Studies and researches have proved that they had communicated through:

- Gestures (hand movements)
- Symbols (drawing the animals)
- Chemical scent (musk glands) – we still have this
- Personal markers (tattoos)
- Physiological changes (blushing)
- Vocal noises (by grunting and shrieking)

They successfully survived in a complex environment only by communicating through their body language. Many of these nonverbal cues still remain a part of our DNA and are wired within our brains. This is the reason we mostly communicate via non-verbal signals mixed with very few verbal cues.

Body language and Psychology

The most important organ of your body is the brain. Without it, nothing is possible. If the brain is dead, we get into vegetative state. Every single organ in your body is controlled by the brain – your eyes, face, hands, legs, heart, legs, etc. It's the same when it comes to nonverbal communications – a constant interaction takes place between the corporal self and the mind.

Since our body language is intertwined with our psyche (the mind), we use corporal behavior to decode what is going on inside our heads. The feelings, intentions, comfort, discomfort and thoughts – all of these happen inside our head.

When you explore nonverbal communication, it is important to do it from the brain's perspective, i.e., to acknowledge that the brain controls all forms of communication. The psychology or the study of the brain should be done from a wider perspective. Understanding body language through human psychology is a complex process. The human brain will have a lot of information to offer – spiritual, cognitive, physiological, emotional and intra-psychic. This approach of analysis helps us to understand the relationship between nonverbal behavior and the psychology behind the same.

When a child is born, it starts to shiver and cry. This behavior triggers the mother to wrap the child in warm clothes to relieve it from the cold. When the child is satisfied with the warmth, the crying stops. This is the first nonverbal message (shivering and crying) a human communicates when he or she comes into this world. This is the start of all the future interactions between the body and the brain.

The next behavior that can be observed in the child is thumb-sucking – he or she learned this in the mother's womb. This is the brain's way to pacify the body – a self-serving behavior. This action may continue for a couple of years. When the child sucks his thumb, he gets pleasure out of it as the brain releases pleasure-inducing endorphins (similar to *opiate* or *opium*). Through this action, the child communicates to the mother that it is currently satisfied.

When the child grows up, it practices many other adaptive behaviors to calm himself during stressful situations. Obvious signs would be biting the lips, chewing gum, touching the lips, biting pen or pencil, etc. Facial stroking, rubbing the neck, playing with the hair are also other - not so obvious - signs. All these signs satisfy the brain's requirement to calm the nerves by releasing endorphins.

The process of communicating our sentiments and needs starts within days of our birth –in the form of smiling, crying, sighing, etc. As the child grows, he will be able to communicate the more complex emotions and needs of the world. Gradually, he will start responding to words (languages), identify the differences in the tone, loudness and speed. He will focus on the eye contact and body posture more than the words – nonverbal signs help him understand better. The psychology of the message depends on the way it is delivered. Consciously and unconsciously, the nonverbal part of the speech remains with us for the rest of our lives.

Power of the human brain

It is surprising that even though we keep using verbal communication on a regular basis, our brain requires us to act physically while expressing sentiments. For instance, when you are excited before you even say anything, you smile or jump out of joy. Happiness, surprise, fear, sadness, anger and disgust are emotions (sentiments), which trigger nonverbal moves from your body. This is universally recognized and accepted.

Children born deaf will develop their own sign language if they do not have adult guidance. The brain helps to create a separate sign language to communicate the complex thoughts that are running within it. This bond between the brain and body language is not unique to humans. It is present in animals as well. The only difference is that our brains have the ability to broadcast more nonverbal information, and not just emotions.

For instance, you look happy, healthy and satisfied when your emotions are in control. The brain ensures you look how you feel. But if your brain or emotions are weak, then the physical appearance sees a drastic change. A homeless person who has schizophrenia will look helpless and sick, owing to the posture, erratic behavior, lack of grooming, etc.

The human body forms a significant communication link with its brain at the time when one is born and this remains active until they die. This link is required to communicate with the outside world as well as to take care of their own needs and desires. Though we have evolved in many ways with each country having its own languages and cultures, we still go back to our primitive habits when we communicate through nonverbal cues (body language).

Be careful while studying the body language and nonverbal behavior of the person as it opens the door to the mind's psychology. The hidden dimensions of the human mind can be found when you closely observe the nonverbal cues.

Interesting facts on Human Psychology

- *We have the tendency to blame a person's behavior on their personality. But when it comes to self - we let it pass.*

Most of us get mad at the behavior of another person under certain circumstances. And the fact is, most people give it back to others by doing the exact same thing minutes later or when the time comes. But when you do it, you tend to justify your action. And when others do it, it is blamed on their personality.

- *This is not a good sign when it comes to predicting our reaction to the future events.*

Most often we think that we are going to react in a particular way to an event that is yet to take place. But when the moment presents itself, our reactions are completely different to what we had predicted. We think that one single instance can change our mood entirely. But when the instance actually happens, it doesn't have the desired effect on us.

- *Our deepest and strongest memories are not really accurate.*

Memories of traumatic events are said to stay strong in our minds forever. These memories are referred as Flashbulb memories. But studies say otherwise. If you were in a strong emotional state when that particular event happened, your memory might be inaccurate. This is because your emotions were running high, and didn't allow you to focus on all the instances of the event. Also, many of our deepest memories and assumptions go back to childhood. As a child, we processed every bit of information given to us as the absolute truth, even if the information given was just a bunch of bull***t.

- *It is possible to concentrate only for ten minutes.*

A person's attention span is limited to ten minutes. If you think you can concentrate on something for more than ten minutes, then it might not be true. According to studies, the human mind begins to wander when the time span crosses ten minutes. How many times would you estimate you lost concentration during this book?

- *Human brains wander about thirty percent of the day.*

We spend close to thirty percent of our day thinking about something or daydreaming. This is the average figure. Some people tend to do it more, and some, less. But researchers say that people who daydream more are creative and better at problem solving.

- *We cannot multitask!*

How often have you heard your colleague saying that *she is good at multitasking*? Certain job requirements mention multitasking as an important criterion for the work profile. But the truth is, *humans cannot multitask*. Yeah, you can listen to music as you work but the brain can process only one high functional task at a time. It simply means either of the following:

- You are either listening to music and ignoring work

- Or you are working and ignoring the music.

It is impossible to think about two tasks at the same time.

- *Decision-making is done at the subconscious level.*

Are you someone who takes a decision after weighing all the options and calculating the impact of the output? But it is not you who is taking the decision; it is your subconscious mind. Your conscious mind will get overwhelmed with a lot of information and might even freeze if all your life's decisions are made at the conscious level. Why is it so? The brain can receive only eleven million bits of information per second. It doesn't have the power to go through all of them in the conscious mind.

- *You need 66 days to form a habit.*

Data from multiple research projects prove that following a particular pattern for 66 days will turn it into a habit. *For instance*: if you continue going to the gym for 66 days, it will become a habit. But you will need to take a conscious effort to do it for 66 days. The absolute duration varies person to person but also depends on the difficulty of the habit.

- *Your brain continues to work even when you sleep.*

There is no change in the mode of the brain when you sleep, i.e., it stays active, just like it was when you are awake. According to scientists, the brain clears all the waste and toxins from the body when you sleep. During the sleep cycle, the brain arranges all the data from the previous day and forms new associations.

- *We choose better with fewer options, even though we keep asking for more choices.*

A simple experiment and research has proved that we are better at choosing when there are less options. Two jam booths were set up for a sale. One booth had six kinds of jam while the other one had 24 kinds of jam. The booth with less options was able to sell **six** times more jam than the other one. This proves another fact we read earlier – *it is impossible for our brain to process too much information.*

It is possible to analyze people if you focus on the hidden signs along with the verbal signals. Concentrate on the person's behavior and try to understand the reason for the same by looking at the patterns. Look for both loud and subtle body language.

Conclusion

We have come to the end of this book. I would like to take this opportunity to thank you once again for choosing this book.

I sincerely hope that this book was useful and helped you, as a reader, to get a clear and in-depth understanding of how to read people. This book will have given a detailed description of the human mind, its behavior, psychology and body language. The chapters concentrate on the variables that need to be focused on while analyzing people.

The book has covered its primary objective - to act as a complete guide to readers who would like to know how to analyze or read people.

It was my pleasure answering the queries you had in mind. For some it might be naturally easier to analyze others but by constant practice anyone can master the art of human psychology. Now go out there and start using the techniques you just learned, responsibly of course! Remember to keep on learning!

Would you mind giving the book a quick review before you go? I'd greatly appreciate it!

Thank you and best wishes!

"human behavior flaws from three main sources: desire, emotion, and knowledge" -- Plato

Additional material

If you liked this book you might be interested on these:

The Power of Habit: Why We Do What We Do and How to Change - by Charles Duhigg

The 48 Laws of Power - by Robert Greene

In addition to everything. You may practice daily meditation to become more conscious and hence increasing the learning curve of what've discussed. Even 5-10 minutes a day is enough to gain all the benefits. If you're interested to learn more about meditation and its benefits you can find a lot of great free information regarding it.

You can also see my eBook on different meditation techniques:

amazon.com/dp/B074WZKW67

Good luck!

Made in the USA
Middletown, DE
31 March 2019